FAIRLY ODD EXCUSES

Based on the TV series *The Fairly OddParents*® as seen on Nickelodeon®

ISBN 0-439-72424-4

12 11 10 9 8 7 6 5 4 3 2 1   5 6 7 8 9 10/0

Printed in the U.S.A.

First Scholastic printing, January 2005

FAIRLY ODD EXCUSES

by David Lewman

SCHOLASTIC INC.

New York   Toronto   London   Auckland   Sydney
Mexico City   New Delhi   Hong Kong   Buenos Aires

TABLE OF CONTENTS

Timmy Explains Excuses 6

Timmy's Excuses for Having the Stuff Wanda and Cosmo
    Give Him 12

Cosmo's Excuses for Getting Timmy in Trouble 14

Wanda's Excuses for Losing Her Wand 16

Excuses Timmy's Dad Uses for Forgetting His
    Wife's Birthday 18

Excuses Timmy's Mom Uses for Hiring Vicky to Babysit 20

Timmy's Excuses for Constantly Playing Video Games 22

Jorgen Von Strangle's Excuses for Skipping
    His Daily Workout 24

Vicky's Excuses for Sending Timmy to Bed Early 26

Mr. Crocker's Excuses for Not Having
    His Pupils' Tests Graded 28

POOF!

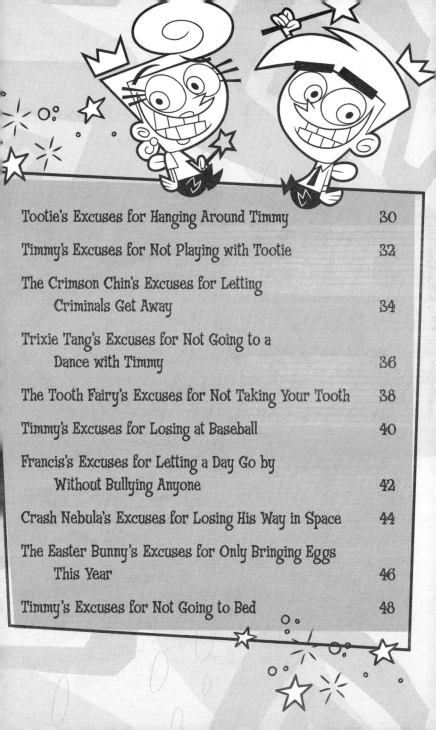

Tootie's Excuses for Hanging Around Timmy — 30

Timmy's Excuses for Not Playing with Tootie — 32

The Crimson Chin's Excuses for Letting
Criminals Get Away — 34

Trixie Tang's Excuses for Not Going to a
Dance with Timmy — 36

The Tooth Fairy's Excuses for Not Taking Your Tooth — 38

Timmy's Excuses for Losing at Baseball — 40

Francis's Excuses for Letting a Day Go by
Without Bullying Anyone — 42

Crash Nebula's Excuses for Losing His Way in Space — 44

The Easter Bunny's Excuses for Only Bringing Eggs
This Year — 46

Timmy's Excuses for Not Going to Bed — 48

Q: What is an excuse?

Cosmo thinks an excuse is something that used to be a cuse.

A: Actually an excuse is a reason you give for doing something. Or not doing something. It should be believable. And it should keep you from getting in trouble.

Q: Why use an excuse?

A: See above line about how they "keep you from getting in trouble."

Q: How do you make up an excuse?

A: First read the examples in this book. They're pretty good excuses. Then think hard. Use your imagination. But don't be *too* imaginative. You want people to believe your excuse. You might even try telling the truth—if it's an emergency.

Q: When do you use an excuse?

A: Anytime someone seems like they're going to be annoyed by what you did. Or mad. Or furious. This seems to happen quite frequently to me.

Q: Where do you use an excuse?

A: Anywhere you want! At school, at home, in Fairy World—excuses come in handy everywhere you go. They're as useful as Fairy Godparents! (Well, almost.)

Q: Who can you give an excuse to?

A: Anyone at all! Parents, teachers, aliens—everyone can use a good excuse now and then.

Warning!

Just like wishes, excuses don't always turn out exactly the way you want them to. Instead of making up excuses, you might just want to tell the truth.

I won a contest for . . . um . . . having the biggest teeth.

I've been extra good this year, so Santa brought me my own spaceship.

It's amazing what you can order from catalogs nowadays.

My parents kind of go nuts over my birthday.

My uncle, whom you never met, is a brilliant inventor. He's very rich . . . and generous.

This dinosaur? It followed me home.

Z-BAY TROPHIES

Um . . . Internet?

13

COSMO'S EXCUSES FOR GETTING TIMMY IN TROUBLE

Wearing this tiny crown makes it hard to think straight.

I didn't know what I was doing! I was crazed with hunger!

I didn't hear his wish because my ears were clogged with fairy wax.

WANDA'S EXCUSES FOR LOSING HER WAND

I left it at the Museum of Sticks.

It slipped out of my fingers after Cosmo used it to stir melted butter.

Timmy's room is such a mess—who can find anything in there?

It's in the shop getting a tune-up.

Goldfish don't have pockets.

I was curling my hair with it-it's Cosmo's fault! 17

EXCUSES TIMMY'S DAD USES FOR FORGETTING HIS WIFE'S BIRTHDAY

I was distracted by National Wear-a-Waffle-on-Your-Head Day.

I thought it was my birthday.

I was too busy getting ready to celebrate the day after your birthday.

I thought you stopped having
birthdays when you were 29!

My calendar was eaten
by squirrels.

Every day is like your birthday
except without a cake and presents!

EXCUSES TIMMY'S MOM USES FOR HIRING VICKY TO BABYSIT

It's my turn to read stories to underprivileged dolphins.

Dad finally remembered to take me out for my birthday.

I have to go buy more food for Timmy's goldfish.

It's parent-teacher conference night, and Mr. Crocker says he has something really important to tell me.

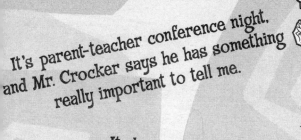

It always looks like Timmy has such a good time with Vicky.

CHA-CHING

Vicky's really cheap. And she really seems to enjoy her job!

Dad and I are going to a lecture called "Spending More Time with Your Child."

TIMMY'S EXCUSES FOR CONSTANTL
PLAYING VIDEO GAMES

My gym teacher said my thumbs need more exercise.

I'm doing a study on the effects of long-term video-game playing.

I'm learning valuable lessons about running, jumping, and grabbing stuff.

JORGEN VON STRANGLE'S EXCUSES FOR SKIPPING HIS DAILY WORKOUT

I was too busy yelling at the newest recruits in the Fairy Academy.

They were all out of the heaviest weights.

Some fairy wished the gym to disappear.

24

VICKY'S EXCUSES FOR SENDING TIMMY TO BED EARLY

The latest studies show that kids need at least sixteen hours of sleep every night.

Timmy refused to shine all thirty pairs of my shoes.

I didn't send him—Timmy just went to bed the second he saw me

Tonight's the night we set our clocks forward six hours.

I told Timmy his bedsheets looked lonely.

Timmy just ate dinner, and if you stay awake with a full stomach, you'll get cramps.

TV—DINNER

I don't need an excuse, twerp–I'M THE BABYSITTER!

27

MR. CROCKER'S EXCUSES FOR NOT HAVING HIS PUPILS' TESTS GRADED

I was too busy building a new fairy-detector.

They don't pay me enough to give you tests and grade them.

Someone made all the tests disappear—someone with a FAIRY GODPARENT!

My F stamp ran out of ink.

I WILL NOT CHASE FAIRIES. I WILL NOT CHASE FAIRIES. I WILL NOT CHASE FAIRIES. I WILL NOT CHASE FAIRIES. I WILL NOT CHASE FAIRIES. I WILL NOT CHASE FAIRIES. I WILL NOT CHASE FAIRIES. I WILL NOT CHASE FAIRIES. I WILL NOT CHASE FAIRIES. I WILL NOT CHASE FAIRIES.

The principal made me write "I WILL NOT CHASE FAIRIES" on the blackboard 1,000 times.

Francis stole my only copy of the answers and wouldn't give it back.

I don't need an excuse— I'M THE TEACHER!

TOOTIE'S EXCUSES FOR HANGING AROUND TIMMY

My sister Vicky hired me as her assistant babysitter.

I'm playing Huck Finn in a school play, so I'm studying how to be a boy.

I'm fascinated by pink baseball hats.

I'm trying to recruit him for my People-Whose-Names-Begin-with-*T* club.

A judge issued an antirestraining order, so I have to be within ten feet of him at all times.

Timmy desperately needs me.

He loves me—he just doesn't know it!

TIMMY'S EXCUSES FOR NOT PLAYING WITH TOOTIE

Sorry, but A. J. needs me to help him with his homework.

Sorry, but Chester needs me to help him play video games.

I'm afraid they ran out of cootie vaccine this year.

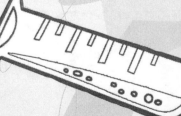

I'm allergic to weird girls.

My mom said I have to rebuild the house.

My dad said I have to make him some waffles to wear on his head.

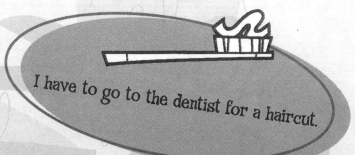

I have to go to the dentist for a haircut.

THE CRIMSON CHIN'S EXCUSES FOR LETTING CRIMINALS GET AWAY

While I was chasing that bad guy I got a terrible cramp in my chin.

If I catch them all, I'll be unemployed.

I slipped on a big word that read "SLIP!"

SLIP!

Even superheroes have to break for lunch.

I figured Mighty Mom and Dyno Dad could handle it.

I'm feeling generous today!

It was Cleft the Boy Chin Wonder's fault!

35

TRIXIE TANG'S EXCUSES FOR NOT GOING TO A DANCE WITH TIMMY

Sorry, I'm having my feet cleaned that day.

My dance shoes don't match your ... anything.

I'm going to the dance with whichever aliens land on Earth that day.

Sorry, but you remind me of someone I'd never go to a dance with-you.

I only go to dances with boys who have limousines, tuxedos, and names that aren't Timmy.

I heard that dance was canceled due to lack of cool boys.

When you're this beautiful, you don't need excuses.

THE TOOTH FAIRY'S EXCUSES FOR NOT TAKING YOUR TOOTH

Sorry, but I was busy celebrating my birthday with Jorgen Von Strangle.

I just paid my taxes, so I ran out of money to leave under your pillow.

Your pillow is stuffed with feathers, and I'm allergic.

38

Fairy World has all the teeth it needs right now.

I took your gum by mistake.

Touching people's teeth is yucky!

I was busy waiting for Timmy Turner to lose his front teeth. I can't wait to get my hands on those big choppers!

 I can't keep up with the late-night hours.

TIMMY'S EXCUSES FOR LOSING AT BASEBALL

The sun got in my eyes.

My dad taught me how to play, and he thought I was on a croquet team.

My fairy godparents can't help me because that's against "Da Rules."

Trixie Tang was watching, so I spent most of the game staring at her.

Every time I was about to catch the ball, Tootie yelled, "I love you, Timmy!"

Running makes me tired!

I'm good, but my glove stinks.

Hey, what do you expect when you're on a team called "The Losers"?

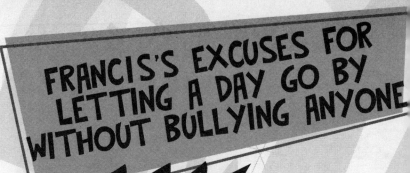

FRANCIS'S EXCUSES FOR LETTING A DAY GO BY WITHOUT BULLYING ANYONE

My arms were sore from beating up everyone the day before.

I was attending a convention for the Big Bullies of America.

6

My mommy said she'd make me cookies if I was nice.

My favorite black T-shirt was in the wash, and I thought I'd look stupid bullying in my *other* black T-shirt.

Once a year I take a one-day vacation from bullying.

All my favorite victims were sick.

I didn't feel like it, okay? What are you going to do—make me?

43

CRASH NEBULA'S EXCUSES FOR LOSING HIS WAY IN SPACE

All the stars look alike to me.

I kept circling around Saturn.

None of the planets ever stay still.

The signs are all millions of light years apart.

My map of the solar system is impossible to fold back up.

My spaceship's compass kept pointing at Planet Magneto.

Houston, I have a problem with directions.

THE EASTER BUNNY'S EXCUSES FOR ONLY BRINGING EGGS THIS YEAR

Have you seen the price of candy lately?

Sugar is too fattening.

I'm sick of trying to clean melted chocolate off the plastic grass.

The Tooth Fairy said if I didn't cut back on the sweets, she'd sell me to a magician.

I got a really good deal on some slightly rotten eggs.

Santa told me that bringing toys is his department.

I lost all the candy in a poker game with Peter Rabbit.

TIMMY'S EXCUSES FOR NOT GOING TO BED

A dog ate my bed.

It's too noisy in my bedroom because my goldfish are having a party.

I can't fall asleep because I'm afraid of Vicky.

My science homework assignment is to stay up all night.

There's a hideous monster under my bed. And a lot of dust.

 Um ... uh ... well ... um ... I **WISH** I COULD THINK OF A GOOD EXCUSE!